NEW VANGUARD 321

ALLIED TANKS AT EL ALAMEIN 1942

WILLIAM E. HIESTAND

ILLUSTRATED BY FELIPE
RODRÍGUEZ

OSPREY PUBLISHING

Bloomsbury Publishing Plc

Kemp House, Chawley Park, Cumnor Hill, Oxford OX2 9PH, UK

29 Earlsfort Terrace, Dublin 2, Ireland

1385 Broadway, 5th Floor, New York, NY 10018, USA

E-mail: info@ospreypublishing.com

www.ospreypublishing.com

OSPREY is a trademark of Osprey Publishing Ltd

First published in Great Britain in 2023

A catalogue record for this book is available from the British Library.

ISBN: PB 9781472858016; eBook 9781472858023

ePDF 9781472858030; XML 9781472858047

23 24 25 26 27 10 9 8 7 6 5 4 3 2 1

Index by Angela Hall
Typeset by PDQ Digital Media Solutions, Bungay, UK
Printed and bound in India by Replika Press Private Ltd.

Title page image:

A line of Sherman tanks The Queen's Bays (2nd Dragoon Guards), 1st Armoured Division, at El Alamein, 24 October 1942.

(© IWM E 18377)

This book is dedicated to my mother and father.

Abbreviations and author's notes

British armoured units were designated regiments, squadrons and troops, and these terms are used throughout this work. Regiments are the equivalent of battalion-sized units in US or German militaries, squadrons are companies and troops are platoons.

AP	armour piercing
DAK	*Deutsches Afrikakorps;* Afrika Korps
HE	high explosive
KRRC	King's Royal Rifle Corps
PAK	*Panzerabwehrkanone* (anti-tank gun)
RB	Rifle Brigade
RTR	Royal Tank Regiment

CONTENTS

ALLIED TANKS AT EL ALAMEIN 1942

INTRODUCTION

The Second Battle of Alamein was the decisive engagement of the North African campaign. Since 1940, the front line had ebbed and flowed hundreds of miles across Libya, with Axis forces twice forced back to El Agheila in western Cyrenaica and twice counter-attacking and driving their Allied opponents eastward. In the summer of 1942, Rommel's *Panzerarmee Afrika* defeated British and Commonwealth forces at Gazala, captured the key port of Tobruk and thrust forward in an audacious bid to capture Alexandria and the Suez Canal. The Eighth Army's desperate stand at the small railway station at Alamein halted Rommel in July, and in August it repelled Rommel's last attempt to outflank Allied defences at the battle of Alam Halfa. Two months later, the Eighth Army's new commander, General Bernard Montgomery, was satisfied that his forces had been adequately trained and equipped to launch their own offensive. After 11 days of intense battle fighting amidst the Axis minefields, the tanks of the Eighth Army broke through and forced Rommel into a retreat that would end with the surrender of over a quarter of a million troops in Tunisia six months later.

Mark VI machine-gun-armed light tanks of the 1st RTR, 7th Armoured Division on patrol in 1940. British armoured units were trained for rapid desert movement and firing on the move, but organization and pre-war doctrine placed little emphasis on combined arms tactics. (Getty Images)

For a battle in North Africa, infantry and artillery played an unusually important role at Second Alamein. The Qattara Depression to the south eliminated the open flank that characterized other desert offensives, and Axis defences consisted of dug-in infantry and anti-tank guns protected by deep minefields that Montgomery attacked with a massive artillery barrage and infantry assault. Nevertheless, as always in the desert the armoured forces played a critical role. Valentine tanks led Eighth Army infantry divisions in the initial assault through the minefields, and British armoured divisions followed closely, driving their own gaps through the minefields. The breakthrough, however, took much longer than planned, and only after days of grinding fighting was a renewed offensive, codenamed *Supercharge*, launched that finally allowed the Eighth Army's tanks to reach the open desert.

The Eighth Army's tank force was larger and better equipped at Second Alamein than at any point in the desert war. Four armoured divisions and two separate brigades fielded over 1,000 tanks containing most of the types used by the British during the North African campaign. In addition to Stuarts, Crusaders and Valentines, the British armoured units crewed US-built M3 Grant and M4 Sherman medium tanks with 75mm guns that at last allowed them to match the Afrika Korps' (DAK) panzers. Tactical and organizational problems that had hindered British armoured operations throughout the desert war persisted at Alamein, however, and Montgomery's armoured divisions struggled to fulfil their assigned role of breaking through and defeating enemy armour. Days of attritional combat by the Eighth Army's tanks, infantry, artillery and air power was needed to grind down Rommel's panzer reserves and, ultimately, drive the Axis to retreat.

Armoured force evolution, organization and doctrine

The Eighth Army's armoured force at Alamein was shaped by decades of pre-war doctrinal debate and repeated defeats at the hands of the Afrika Korps. During the inter-war years, military theorists such as J.F.C. Fuller and B.H. Liddell Hart argued that tanks would decide future campaigns with only minimal support from other arms, and this 'tank-dominant' school shaped British organization and tactics early in the war. In Egypt, General Percy

An Afrika Korps column moving through Libya in 1941. Rommel's panzer divisions operated as concentrated combined arms units and inflicted repeated defeats on their British opponents after being dispatched by Hitler to shore up the Italians. (Getty Images)

Hobart formed and led the 7th 'Desert Rats' Armoured Division in accordance with Fuller and Liddell Hart's precepts before Italy entered the war, training it to conduct sweeping manoeuvres through the desert with tank-heavy units. Due to the threat of air attack, British tanks were to move dispersed and then rapidly concentrate against the enemy's flanks or rear. The tank-on-tank clash was expected to decide future battles, and the 7th trained for operations resembling naval warfare, with movements in line and column, broadsides and even crossing the enemy's 'T'. The British expected that firing on the move, for which they trained extensively, would give them an edge. Hobart felt that infantry or artillery would only slow down his fast-moving armour, and little emphasis was placed on combined arms training.

The organization of the British armoured division in 1940 reflected the tank-dominant approach. It was tank heavy, with a table of organization strength of 330 cruiser and light tanks in six tank regiments organized in two tank brigades. There was little tactical role for the two motor rifle infantry battalions and artillery in the division's support group aside from providing a night harbour for the tanks to refuel and rearm. Further complicating armoured division operations was the tendency to disperse what limited infantry and artillery was available in small 'Jock Columns'. Named for their creator, Jock Campbell, the commander of the 7th's Support Group, they typically consisted of a company of motorized infantry, a battery of 25-pdr field guns, and small detachments of anti-tank guns and armoured cars. Jock columns could be useful for scouting, screening and raiding operations, and were favoured by junior officers as they allowed for independent command, but as the desert war went on it was realized they dispersed and fragmented combat power, especially divisional artillery. Hobart was removed from command before operations began, but his tank-centric approach seemed to be validated as the 7th Armoured played a leading role in the Operation *Compass* offensive that rapidly outmanoeuvred and destroyed Italian forces in 1940.

The flaws in British armoured organization and doctrine came into sharp focus with the arrival of Erwin Rommel and the lead elements of the Afrika Korps in early 1941. In short order, Rommel attacked from El Agheila, destroyed the British 2nd Armoured Division and encircled Tobruk. German panzer divisions were fully integrated combined arms units that, unlike their opponents, operated in compact formations, tightly integrating the employment of their tanks, artillery, infantry and anti-tank guns. British tanks struggling to fulfil their role of engaging their panzer counterparts were repeatedly lured to charge screens of anti-tank guns, and many losses attributed to enemy tanks were actually due to the Panzerabwehrkanone (PAK; anti-tank guns). The German standard 50mm anti-tank gun was effective against British tank armour and the deadly 88mm dual-purpose gun proved a lethal tank-killer at long range. Lacking an effective high-explosive (HE) shell for their 2-pdr main armament, and with little ability to support tanks with infantry and artillery, the Eighth Army's armoured units proved unable to cope with their Axis opponents.

Two armour-led attempts to relieve Tobruk, Operations *Brevity* and *Battleaxe*, failed at the hands of the Afrika Korps, and Sir Claude Auchinleck, newly appointed Middle East commander in chief, built up a strong tank force to launch Operation *Crusader* in December 1941. Although ultimately successful in relieving Tobruk, the offensive revealed continuing shortcomings in the Eighth Army's approach to mobile operations. The 7th Armoured Division was assigned three full armoured brigades along with its small support group for the offensive, resulting in a large, unwieldy force of 450 tanks. The brigades became scattered and repeatedly took heavy losses in isolated engagements with concentrated German and Italian armoured units. Tactically, panzer units continued to refrain from closing with British armour, lingering at long range and shelling their opponents with HE. Lacking the ability to respond and needing to close the range to be able to penetrate enemy tank armour, British tanks were often goaded into tank charges and lured by the panzers into screens of anti-tank guns.

Stuart tanks of the 4th Armoured Brigade training in August 1941, demonstrating the dispersed formations typically used by the British to minimize the impact of air attack. During Operation *Crusader* in late 1941, the Eighth Army succeeded in relieving Tobruk and driving Rommel back to El Agheila, but organizational and tactical shortfalls led to heavy losses to British armour. (Getty Images)

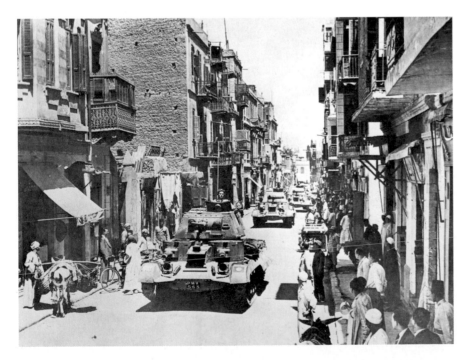

British A9 Cruisers of the 7th Armoured Division in Cairo before the beginning of operations against Italian forces in Libya, 1940. Pre-war A9, A10 and A13 cruisers were fast but unreliable and poorly armoured. These early tanks largely left the Eighth Army's order of battle after Operation *Crusader*. (Getty Images)

Despite ultimately driving Rommel from the field, losses to the armour were so heavy that the British realized more combined arms integration was needed. The tank-heavy armoured division was transformed in early 1942 into a more balanced organization, with one armoured and one motorized infantry brigade. The new structure resulted in an armoured brigade of three tank regiments and one motorized infantry battalion, and a motorized brigade with three additional infantry battalions. German panzer divisions were adept at rapidly forming Kampfgruppen – battlegroups – with mixes of tanks, artillery and infantry tailored to the tactical needs of the day. Seeking similar combined arms integration at the tactical level, in the Middle East the Eighth Army directed a more rigid approach, creating what were termed brigade groups by permanently attaching infantry, artillery and anti-tank units to each armoured brigade.

These were steps in the right direction, and with the arrival of US M3 Grant medium tanks with 75mm guns in early 1942, British forces began to prepare for an offensive with some optimism. However, Rommel struck first in late May and in several weeks of intense fighting inflicted a crushing defeat on the Eighth Army at Gazala. Army, corps and division levels of command were unable to cope with the speed of Axis operations. Armoured brigades were again defeated in isolation by the concentrated German panzer divisions or shattered in unsupported tank charges, while the infantry was left isolated in fortified boxes surrounded by minefields on the Gazala line. The battle at Knightsbridge was the final catastrophe for British armour, which suffered crippling losses to Axis tanks and anti-tank guns. Rommel rapidly followed with the capture of Tobruk and 32,000 prisoners on 21 June. Despite the new armoured brigade group and division organizations, British tank units were still often scattered across the battlefield and defeated in detail. The decentralized brigade group concept removed most of the artillery and anti-tank assets from divisional control, leaving the division

CRUSADER II

1. A Crusader II of the 9th Lancers, 2nd Armoured Brigade, 1st Armoured Division, 23 October 1942. The 2nd Brigade had a mix of tanks totalling 29 Crusader IIs, 39 Crusader IIIs and 92 Shermans. At the beginning of the battle, 105 of the X Corps' 441 tanks were Crusader IIs despite the limitations of the tank's obsolete 2-pdr main armament. Note the forward small Besa machine-gun turret that was rarely manned in combat. British tanks in early 1942 were typically painted in overall sand scheme, but at Alamein, they were usually painted with a dark green camouflage pattern over the basic sand. British tanks also carried a wide variety of formation and additional markings: visible on this Crusader is the War Department Census Number on the turret side, an individual number assigned to each vehicle. Tank Census Numbers all began with 'T'. The 1st Armoured Division was heavily engaged during Operation *Lightfoot* and later was reinforced by the 10th Armoured Division's 8th Armoured Brigade to participate in the *Supercharge* attack on 2 November. The division failed to move rapidly enough to exploit the 9th Armoured Brigade's costly attack but inflicted heavy losses on Rommel's counter-attacking mobile divisions, forcing Axis forces to abandon the Alamein area on the 4th.

2. A Crusader III of the 2nd Armoured Brigade, 1st Armoured Division. The British realized that the Crusader's 2-pdr was obsolete by 1942, and fielded a new variant, the Crusader III, equipped with the 6-pdr (57mm). The new gun gave British crews the ability to penetrate the improved armour of German tanks, although the size of the gun reduced the room in the turret. The turret crew consisted of the gunner and a commander who additionally had to load the 6-pdr. As the front Besa machine-gun turret was removed, and the space used for storing additional ammunition for the 6-pdr, the tank was left with a total crew of three. Crusader IIIs began to reach the Eighth Army in appreciable numbers by October 1942, and 66 served in the battle along with 154 Crusader IIs at the beginning of Operation *Lightfoot*.

1

2

A British tank crew cleaning the barrel of its Crusader's 2-pdr in February 1942. The Eighth Army built up a large armoured force in 1942, but suffered a major defeat at the Gazala line that led to the fall of Tobruk and retreat to Alamein. (Getty Images)

HQ as an administrative command unable to adequately reinforce, support and orchestrate the operations of its subordinate brigades.

After a brief stand at Mersa Matruh followed by a chaotic withdrawal, Auchinleck assumed personal command of the Eighth Army and was at last able to halt the triumphant but exhausted and overextended Panzerarmee Afrika at Alamein in early July. Sensing an opportunity to crush Rommel's weakened forces, Auchinleck launched his battered forces into a series of uncoordinated and costly attacks against Axis positions for the next several weeks. The Eighth Army attacks were crippled by its inability to integrate tank and infantry operations. Again and again, night infantry assaults would seize their objectives, but British armour would fail to move forward in support, leaving the attackers to be overrun by German panzer counter-attacks the next day. Trust between the Eighth Army's armour and its infantry, in particular the Commonwealth division commanders, collapsed.

The appointment of General Bernard Montgomery to command the Eighth Army on 13 August brought firm control at the army level. He insisted divisions be employed as coherent units to maintain control and mass firepower, and the decentralized Jock Columns and armoured brigade groups were abolished. Rather than disperse combat power, Montgomery wanted to mass it with the formation of what he termed a *corps de chasse,* an armour-heavy corps able to match and defeat the panzers of the Afrika Korps. Before he could reshape the Eighth Army for the offensive, however, Montgomery faced Rommel's last attack on 30 August. Axis forces penetrated British minefields on the southern portion of the Alamein line but were delayed by the Desert Air Force and the light armoured elements of the 7th Armoured Division. With limited fuel, the Panzerarmee shifted its axis of attack north earlier than planned and hit Alam Halfa Ridge, laced with Eighth Army tanks, infantry and anti-tank guns. The attackers were repulsed, with 113 tanks damaged and 38 abandoned on the battlefield; the Eighth Army lost 67 tanks. Montgomery did not consider his forces adequately trained to meet the panzer divisions in open manoeuvre combat and did not pursue.

The defensive success at Alam Halfa was followed by weeks of intensive reorganization, re-equipping and training as Montgomery prepared to launch his own offensive, designated Operation *Lightfoot.* Montgomery formed his 1st and 10th Armoured Divisions into the tank-heavy X Corps to serve as his equivalent to the Afrika Korps' 15th and 21st Panzer Divisions. New supplies flooded in, including over 300 M4 Sherman tanks and 100 M7 Priest 105mm self-propelled howitzers from the United States. Montgomery insisted on a programme of intensive training, and divisions and brigades were constantly rotated from the front line for drills and exercises. As the Eighth Army's initial challenge was breaking through dug-in defences protected by deep minefields, the training focused on penetrating fortified positions and minefields rather than manoeuvre or pursuit.

October 1942: The Eighth Army order of battle

When ready for the offensive in late October, Montgomery's army consisted of seven infantry and four armoured divisions. Unlike Rommel's forces, the Eighth Army experienced continued organizational turbulence during the desert war, with units and commanders constantly arriving and departing; only four of the divisions at Second Alamein had fought at Gazala, while another four were completely new to the desert. Montgomery organized his forces under three corps headquarters. The XIII Corps under LtGen Brian Horrocks, a Montgomery protégé new to the desert, held the southern portion of the front with the 44th and 50th Infantry and 7th Armoured Divisions. Sir Oliver Leese's XXX Corps launched the main attack with, from north to south, the 9th Australian, 51st Highland, 2nd New Zealand and 1st South African Divisions, while his 4th Indian covered the corps front further south. Montgomery had placed the 1st and 10th Armoured Divisions under the X Corps – his *corps de chasse* – and, despite misgivings, had left LtGen Herbert Lumsden, a desert veteran, in command.

Crusader IIs advancing at speed. The Crusader's 340hp engine and Christie suspension gave it good speed, but its light armour, poor reliability and 2-pdr gun remained disadvantages. (Getty Images)

While the infantry divisions included four units from the Commonwealth, the four armoured divisions were all British manned. The 1st, 7th and 10th Armoured Divisions controlled a total of four armoured and one light armoured brigade; the 8th Armoured had its brigades detached and did not fight in the engagement as a division. A separate armoured brigade was assigned to support the XXX Corps infantry divisions in the assault and another was directly attached to the 2nd New Zealand Division. In total, the Eighth Army controlled 21 armoured regiments with over 1,000 tanks, while another 200 tanks were held ready to replace losses.

Eighth Army tank holdings, 23 October 1942	
Shermans	252
Grants	170
Crusaders	294
Stuarts	119
Valentines	194
Scorpions	24
Churchills	6
Total	**1,059**
Reserve tanks	200

The British armoured division table of organization in October 1942 included one armoured and one motorized infantry brigade, along with reconnaissance, artillery and various support units held at division level. The armoured brigade contained three armoured regiments and a motorized

Crusader IIIs advance at El Alamein. The Crusader III lacked the front machine-gun turret of the Crusader II and carried a 6-pdr main gun in place of the Crusader II's 2-pdr. (Getty Images)

infantry battalion. Armoured regiments at full strength had over 50 tanks, typically with two squadrons of Grants or Shermans and a third light squadron of Crusaders. The armoured brigade's motorized battalion was tactically mounted, with each infantry section carried in its own transport, usually a 15cwt truck, to allow for rapid dismounting. Motorized battalions were also equipped with 16 6-pdr (57mm) anti-tank guns, a major improvement on the previous 2-pdrs. The Eighth Army contained only a single motorized brigade in October, the 7th, assigned to the 1st Armoured Division for the offensive with its three motorized battalions. As the other armoured divisions lacked motorized infantry brigades, the 44th Infantry Division's 131st was assigned to the 7th Armoured and the 133rd to the 10th before *Lightfoot*. These were re-designated as lorried infantry brigades – retaining their standard infantry organization but assigned enough organic transport to move the entire formation. Unlike the motorized battalions, their lorried infantry battalions lacked the 16 6-pdr anti-tank guns and were carried in larger trucks that mounted platoons rather than the section-carrying 15cwts. The transfer of the 44th's infantry brigades to the armoured divisions took place shortly before the battle, allowing little time for integrated training between the armoured and lorried infantry brigades.

X Corps tank order of battle, 23 October 1942				
Unit	Grants	Shermans	Crusader IIs	Crusader IIIs
X Corps HQ	2			
1st Armoured Division HQ			8	
2nd Armoured Brigade/1st AD	1	92	39	29
10th Armoured Division HQ			7	
8th Armoured Brigade/10th AD	57	31	33	12
24th Armoured Brigade/10th AD	2	93	28	17
Total	**62**	**216**	**115**	**58**

Lumsden's X Corps consisted of the 1st and 10th Armoured and the 2nd New Zealand Infantry Division, although the New Zealanders were attached to XXX Corps for the initial *Lightfoot* assault. The 1st was commanded by

Crusader IIIs on the move, highlighting the tank's sleek design and sloped turret armour. The Crusader had an effective Christie suspension that allowed for good cross-country mobility, although the large springs took up a great amount of the tank's internal space. (Getty Images)

MajGen Raymond Briggs and had served in the desert since early 1942. Its defeat at Knightsbridge led directly to the fall of Tobruk and the retreat of the Eighth Army into Egypt. At Mersa Matruh and First Alamein, command confusion and turbulence contributed to several occasions where the 1st's tanks were unable to support infantry units under attack, leading to the breakdown of trust between Eighth Army infantry and armour.

The 1st Armoured was withdrawn for rebuilding after the July fighting on the Alamein line and was not present during Alam Halfa. It returned well equipped, with 92 Shermans and one of its artillery regiments equipped with 105mm Priest self-propelled howitzers. It entered action on 23 October with the 2nd Armoured and 7th Motorized Brigades. The 2nd consisted of three armoured regiments: the Queen's Bays, 9th Lancers and 10th Hussars, each with a squadron with approximately 16 Crusader IIs and IIIs, and two squadrons of 15 M4A1 Sherman tanks. The Yorkshire Dragoon motorized battalion, with 16 6-pdr anti-tank guns, completed the 2nd Armoured Brigade, and the 7th Motorized Brigade contained three additional motorized battalions – the 2nd Kings Royal Rifle Corps and the 2nd and 7th Battalions of the Rifle Brigade. The division also contained Hammerforce, a special task force that consisted of the 8th Armoured Division's headquarters controlling armoured car, anti-tank and anti-aircraft elements. As each of the X Corps armoured divisions were to clear their own paths through the minefields, the 1st created a task force of three engineer companies covered by the 7th Brigade's 2nd Rifle Brigade (RB) motor rifle battalion and a tank platoon from each of the 2nd Armoured's armoured regiments.

Crusader IIs in Tunisia after the battle of the Mareth line in 1943. Crusaders continued to serve as front-line tanks throughout the Tunisian campaign, but afterwards were replaced by Shermans in British armoured units in Sicily and Italy. The Crusader chassis was adopted for other purposes, including an anti-aircraft tank variant carrying two 20mm Oerlikon AA guns. (Getty Images)

Local defence volunteer officers from the Middlesex battalion examine a US M3 Grant and an M3 Stuart at a tank training centre in England in July 1942. The confusing US designation of both tanks as 'M3' led the British to assign American Civil War generals' names to US tanks. (Getty Images)

Lumsden's X Corps' second armoured division was the 10th, formed from the 1st Cavalry Division. The 1st began the war posted in Palestine, and participated in operations in Iraq, Syria and Iran in 1941 with its cavalry squadrons mounted in trucks. The 1st was subsequently ordered to re-equip as an armoured division but received few tanks for training. Re-designated the 10th Armoured, the division was transferred to the Eighth Army in the autumn of 1942 and MajGen Alexander Gatehouse, an experienced desert hand, took command. On 23 October, the 10th consisted of the 8th and 24th Armoured Brigades and the 133rd Lorried Infantry Brigade. The new division accordingly resembled the tank-heavy 1941 organization with two armoured brigades, but of the six armoured regiments and five infantry battalions in the division, only the 3rd Royal Tank Regiment (RTR) and two infantry battalions had previous desert combat experience. Unlike the

B   **STUART M3 AND MK I.**

1. A Stuart M3 light tank of the Scots Greys, 4th Light Armoured Brigade, 7th Armoured Division. The 4th had been a mixed Grant and Stuart unit at the battle of Gazala but, after heavy losses, had been re-formed with armoured car regiments and the 4/8th Hussars with Stuarts. By the time of Second Alamein, the brigade had the 4/8th with 48 Stuarts, the Scots Greys with 16 Stuarts and 14 Grants along with the two armoured car units. This 4th Brigade Stuart has the famous 'Desert Rat' divisional Jerboa symbol on its left fender, and the 40 in the red square identifies the tank's regiment as the Scots Greys. The 4th had capably screened the southern portion of the Alamein line since July. During Second Alamein, the 7th Armoured was moved into army reserve before *Supercharge*, and the 4th was ultimately attached to the 2nd New Zealand Division to replace the heavily damaged 9th Armoured Brigade.

2. A Stuart Mk I of the 2nd New Zealand Division Cavalry Regiment, October 1942. Designed in the US as a light tank, the Stuart had a combination of firepower, mobility and armour similar to the Crusader II and it was initially deployed by the Eighth Army in the cruiser tank role in 1941. Although its range was limited, the tank was so mechanically reliable that it was dubbed the 'Honey' in North Africa by crews used to breakdown-prone British cruisers. With the arrival of Grants and, later in 1942, Shermans, the Stuart was relegated to its original light tank role. In XXX Corps, five Stuarts were in the 9th Australian Division's cavalry squadron, and 25 in the New Zealand division's along with several attached to the divisional headquarters. The New Zealand Stuarts were painted in a simple overall sand finish. The Eighth and First Armies continued to employ Stuarts in Tunisia. Upgraded but still with weak armour and only a 37mm gun, Stuarts continued to be employed throughout the war as the Allies' primary tracked reconnaissance vehicle.

1

2

A crewman gains the highest visibility possible from his Stuart while another mans the .30cal Browning machine gun on the anti-aircraft pintle mount. Stuarts were used for scouting and screening missions at Alamein during the summer and autumn of 1942, as enough Crusaders, Grants and Shermans had arrived to fill the main battle tank role. (Getty Images)

1st Armoured Division, the 10th did not attach infantry or armoured elements to the three engineer companies and one separate platoon of its mine-clearing detachment.

The 10th's 8th Armoured Brigade consisted of the 3rd RTR, Sherwood Rangers and Staffordshire Yeomanry armoured regiments equipped with a total of 57 Grants, 31 Shermans, 33 Crusader IIs and 12 6-pdr-equipped Crusader IIIs. The 1st Battalion of the Buffs served as the brigade motorized infantry battalion. The 24th Armoured Brigade was more heavily equipped with the new Shermans in its 41st, 45th and 47th RTR regiments, totalling two Grants, 93 Shermans and 45 Crusaders. The 11th Battalion of the King's Royal Rifle Corps (KRRC) served as the brigade motor infantry battalion. The 133rd was detached from the 44th Infantry Division and attached to the 10th to serve as its lorried infantry brigade.

The 8th Armoured Division was formed in Britain in 1941 with Matildas and Valentines as no cruiser tanks were available, and alerted for transfer to the Middle East in April 1942. Its 23rd Armoured Brigade arrived first and was rapidly deployed in the last days of the First Battle of Alamein for Operation *Splendour,* an ill-considered charge against enemy positions that resulted in the loss of 44 per cent of its personnel and 93 of its 106 tanks. Even with the arrival of the 24th Armoured Brigade, the 8th never operated as a full division in combat as it lacked an infantry brigade, and the experienced 1st and 7th Armoured Division headquarters were available to control the armoured brigades in theatre. The 24th was re-equipped with Grants and Crusaders and attached to the 10th Armoured Division for the *Lightfoot* offensive, while the 23rd, with replacement Valentine tanks, went to XXX Corps to support the initial infantry assault. The 8th Armoured Division headquarters was formally disbanded on 1 January 1943.

XIII Corps contained the most famous armoured division of the war, the 7th Desert Rats. The 7th had fought in the desert since the first engagements with the Italians in 1940, and would subsequently battle through Tunisia, Italy, France and into Germany. The 7th had lost heavily in the initial phase of the Gazala battle, and during the summer the weakened division was assigned to screen the southern portion of the Alamein line with its 7th Motorized Brigade and its 4th Armoured Brigade organized as a light armoured formation with Stuarts in the 4/8th Hussar regiment and two armoured car regiments. The division created mixed tank and armoured car columns with elements of the motorized rifle brigade to screen the minefields, and at Alam Halfa delayed and harassed the advance and withdrawal of Rommel's forces.

By 23 October, the 4th Light Armoured consisted of the Scots Greys and 4/8th Hussars with a total of 67 Stuarts and 14 Grants, two armoured car

A Stuart refuels during the pursuit after Second Alamein. While reliable and fast, the Stuart's radial engine and smaller fuel capacity gave the tank a limited range of around 110km. As a result, Stuart tank crews generally tried to refuel every 20 miles to be ready for combat manoeuvres. (Getty Images)

regiments and the 1st KRRC motor infantry battalion. The 7th Armoured Division's primary striking power was provided by the newly assigned 22nd Armoured Brigade, containing the 1st and 5th RTR, 4th County of London Yeomanry and a motor battalion, the 1st RB. As the 7th was assigned a secondary mission for Operation *Lightfoot*, it did not receive any of the new M4 Shermans and relied on its 71 Grant M3 mediums and eight 6-pdr-equipped Crusader IIIs for heavy firepower against German tanks and anti-tank guns. The 7th Motorized Brigade had been previously transferred to the 1st Armoured Division, and the 7th received the 131st Infantry Brigade from the 44th Division to serve as a lorried infantry brigade in its place.

XIII Corps tank order of battle, 23 October 1942				
Unit	Grants	Crusader IIs	Crusader IIIs	Stuarts
XIII Corps				
7th Armoured Division HQ		7		
4th Light Armoured Brigade/7th Armoured Division	14			67
22nd Armoured Brigade/7th Armoured Division	57	42	8	19
Total	**71**	**49**	**8**	**86**

The 23rd Armoured Brigade supported the XXX Corps infantry assault with four regiments equipped with Valentines. Regiments were assigned to support the 9th Australian, 51st Highland and 1st South African Infantry Divisions for the initial *Lightfoot* attack, and the fourth retained in reserve. While the 23rd Brigade was equipped with Valentines, designed as a replacement for the Matilda 'I' tank, it had been raised and trained as a cruiser brigade as part of the 8th Armoured Division. Arriving in the Middle East ahead of the other divisional elements, it was rushed into the disastrous Operation *Splendour* assault at the conclusion of First Alamein,

A local defence volunteer drives a US M3 medium tank in training in Britain. This tank is in the original US configuration, designated General Lee by the British. Such tanks had the radio in the hull and a seven-man crew. The British requested a redesigned turret with the radio installed behind the gunner and the turret machine gun mounted coaxially with the 37mm, and these variants were termed General Grants. (Getty Images)

losing most of its tanks to mines and anti-tank guns in a matter of minutes. Rebuilt, the 23rd was assigned an infantry support role better suited to its Valentine tanks, although it maintained some aspects of the armoured brigade organization including an organic motorized rifle battalion, the 11th KRRC. The 23rd also received a self-propelled artillery regiment with 16 self-propelled artillery Bishops carrying 25-pdrs.

XXX Corps, 23rd Armoured Brigade tank order of battle, 23 October		
Unit	Number of Valentine tanks	Comments
8 RTR	51	Supported 1 SA Div, 23 Oct
40 RTR	42	Supported 9 Aus Div, 23 Oct
46 RTR	49	Initially in reserve, supported 9 Aus Div, 28/29 Oct
50 RTR	44	Supported 51 H Div, 23 Oct
Total	**186**	

Formally part of the X Corps, the 2nd New Zealand Division was attached to XXX Corps to participate in the initial *Lightfoot* assault on 23 October. Division commander General Bernard Freyberg had lost all faith in British armour, having seen his battalions repeatedly overrun while nearby tanks failed to move up in support. As a result, he had withdrawn his 4th Brigade to be re-formed as a New Zealand-manned armoured brigade. In the interim, Montgomery agreed to give Freyberg the 9th Armoured Brigade to serve as an organic element of the division for *Lightfoot*. The 9th had been formed from elements of the 1st Cavalry Division in Palestine, and when it moved to Egypt in May 1942, it received a full set of Crusader IIs and IIIs, Grants and Shermans. It operated during the battle with the 14th Battalion Sherwood Foresters as its motorized infantry battalion, along with the 4th Field Regiment, New Zealand Artillery with 24 25-pdrs as its attached artillery support.

9th Armoured Brigade tank order of battle, 23 October 1942			
Unit	Crusader II and IIIs	Grants	Shermans
9th Armoured HQ	3		1
3rd King's Own Hussars	16	9	12
Royal Wiltshire Yeomanry	18	12	8
Warwickshire Yeomanry	17	14	13
Total	**54**	**35**	**34**

TECHNICAL FACTORS

The Eighth Army's tanks suffered from significant shortcomings, although they were not as inferior to their Axis opponents as thought at the time. Mechanical reliability was critical to tank operations in the desert, and the early-war A-9, A-10, A-13 and 1941 Crusader cruisers, as well as the Matilda infantry support tank, were all notoriously unreliable. Mechanical breakdowns in an engagement often cost the Eighth Army more tanks than enemy fire. In the open terrain of the desert, gun power and range were also vital and the British main tank armament through early 1942 was the QF 2-pdr (40mm), a capable anti-tank gun when first fielded in the late 1930s. The round was relatively small and could be held in one hand, and even if it penetrated an enemy tank several hits might be needed to cause disabling damage. The 2-pdr could also be fired as the tank was on the move – a capability valued by early-war British tankers – with a shoulder pad that allowed the gunner to manually adjust the elevation of the gun. The 2-pdr lacked the ability to fire HE shells, however, leaving British tanks unable to deal with enemy anti-tank guns or other soft targets. Further, by 1942 the 2-pdr's anti-armour performance was eroding as the Germans either case hardened or added additional plate to their PzKpfw (Panzerkampfwagen) III and IV armour, forcing British tanks with 2-pdrs to close the range to 500 yards or less.

In addition to armour upgrades, the German PzKpfw IIIs and IVs had larger turret rings that accommodated longer and more powerful versions of their 50mm and 75mm guns. In contrast, limitations imposed on British designers to accommodate rail transportation in Britain made their tanks difficult to up-gun or up-armour, as the turret ring sizes were small and the engines could not support much additional weight. Only the arrival of the US Grants and, in time for Second Alamein, M4 Shermans finally allowed British tank units to meet their German rivals on even terms.

A Grant with the modified turret with wireless on the left, and an unmodified Lee on the right. The Eighth Army predominantly used the Grant variant with a six-man crew, but losses led to the use of some Lees with a seventh man needed to operate the wireless in the hull. These Grants and Lees are equipping 'C' Squadron, 4th (Queen's Own) Hussars, 2nd Armoured Brigade, 7 July 1942, during the desperate fighting to halt Rommel at Alamein. (© IWM E 14053)

Composition of the British tank force in North Africa, 1941–42

Type	*Battleaxe* (June 1941)	*Crusader* (Nov 1941)	Gazala (May 1942)	Alam Halfa (Aug 1942)	Second Alamein (Oct 1942)
Churchills					6
Shermans					252
Grants			167	164	170
Stuarts		198	149	169	119
Valentines		~60	167	163	194
Crusaders	53	210	257	197	294
Matildas	92	~130	110	–	24 (Scorpions)
Early cruisers (A9, 10, 13)	38	126	–	–	–
Total tanks	**183**	**~724**	**850**	**693**	**1,059**

A Grant passes a knocked-out German Panzer I light tank in June 1942. The arrival of Grants in 1942 with their 75mm main armament gave Eighth Army tank crews a major boost in morale, as they felt they finally had a weapon that gave them the means to meet German panzers on even terms. (© IWM E 12920)

Cruisers and Crusaders

Britain fielded pre-war A9, A10 and A13 cruiser tanks in the desert in 1940, along with large numbers of machine-gun-equipped Mark VI light tanks; dwindling numbers of these tanks served through 1941. All three cruiser models were lightly armoured, speedy, mechanically unreliable and equipped with the 2-pdr. In 1941, the new A15 Crusader II cruiser tank arrived. The Crusader featured a low, sleek design with angled turret armour, and became the Allied tank most popularly associated with the desert war. Unfortunately, the Crusader was hastily designed in 1939–40 before wartime lessons could be incorporated, suffered many teething problems, and proved to be only a limited improvement on the pre-war cruisers.

The Crusader II had a 340-horsepower (hp) US V-12 Liberty engine originally designed for aircraft during World War I, along with a Christie suspension that gave good mobility and a top off-road speed of 24km/hr. Fully fuelled, the tank had a cruising range of 320km. As was typical of a British cruiser design, armour was light, 49mm on the gun mantlet and 30mm on the hull front, although the sloped armour on the turret and the tank's overall low profile improved protection. Crusaders were vulnerable to fire and explosion when hit due to the cordite in stored ammunition; not ignition of the petrol fuel as was widely believed at the time. The turret was designed for three men, allowing the ideal gunner, loader and commander arrangement. The

Crusader was fielded with a coaxial-mounted Besa machine gun alongside the 2-pdr, and an additional Besa in a small forward turret. The forward Besa turret proved so hot and vulnerable that it was usually left unmanned in the desert, reducing the typical overall Crusader crew from five to four.

The Crusader II carried the same 40mm 2-pdr main gun as all early British tanks, and the lack of an HE capability left the Crusaders helpless against German anti-tank guns or other soft targets. By mid-1942, the improved German armour on the PzKpfw IIIs and IVs limited the effectiveness of the 2-pdr against enemy tanks. As with the earlier cruiser designs, a close support (CS) variant of the Crusader was fielded with a 3in. howitzer in place of the 2-pdr, with one to two typically assigned to the squadron headquarters element. While the 3in. howitzer could lob HE shells out to over 900 metres, such ammunition was in short supply, and the limited number of 'CS' Crusaders were usually confined to firing smoke shells to try and cover tank movements. Above all, the Crusader suffered from poor mechanical reliability. Despite efforts to prepare Crusaders for desert operations when they arrived in the theatre, the tank suffered from chronic maintenance issues due to inadequate externally mounted air filters that quickly clogged and a chain-driven fan that rapidly wore out. More Crusaders were out of action due to breakdowns than enemy action.

British designers developed the Crusader III in 1942, with the turret modified to carry the more powerful 57mm 6-pdr main gun. The 57mm had much improved anti-armour capabilities and could fire a small HE shell. As the British still placed emphasis on firing on the move, much of the new gun was balanced inside the turret to allow the gunner to manually change elevation with a shoulder pad as with the 2-pdr. The large gun breach left no room for the three-man crew of the Crusader II, and the commander had to also serve as the loader, hindering the effective operation of the tank in action. The forward small Besa machine-gun turret was also removed, and the space used for storing additional 6-pdr ammunition. With the gunner now also assigned to work the wireless, the tank had a three-man crew, down from the Crusader II's four or five, reducing the number of personnel available for daily maintenance, refuelling and ammunition reloading.

Crusaders arrived as a major part of Churchill's Tiger Cubs convoy in 1941 but proved disappointing in their first action during Operation *Battleaxe* in 1941, with many lost due to breakdowns. During Operation *Crusader* the Crusader was the Eighth Army's main battle tank, completely equipping the 7th Armoured's 7th and 22nd Armoured Brigades. The arrival of US M3 Grant medium tanks with 75mm guns in mid-1942 led the Eighth

Grants of the 5th Royal Tank Regiment manoeuvre in column in February 1942. After the huge losses in British armour at Gazala and Knightsbridge, the remaining Grants were carefully husbanded to defend the Alamein position as the Eighth Army felt they were the only means of halting Rommel's thrust into Egypt. (Getty Images)

Army to reorganize its armoured regiments to consist of two light squadrons with Stuarts or Crusaders along with a nine-tank squadron of Grants. By late October 1942, enough US medium tanks had arrived to allow the typical armoured regiment to have two squadrons of either M3 Grants or M4 Shermans and one light squadron of Crusaders. Crusader IIs and IIIs joined in the pursuit after Alamein and fought in Tunisia, but the tank was declared obsolete in 1943, and Shermans, later joined by British-designed Cromwells and Comets, equipped British armoured divisions for the remainder of the war. The Crusader chassis was used through the rest of the war for a variety of other purposes, in particular anti-aircraft tanks.

Tank characteristics

	Crusader II	M3 Stuart I	M3 Grant	M4A1 Sherman	Valentine III	Churchill III
Crew	4–5	4	6	5	4	5
Weight (metric tons)	19.3	12.7	28.1	30.3	17.3	40
Horsepower (hp)	340 at 1,500rpm	262 at 2,400rpm	350–400 at 2,400rpm	400–460 at 2,400rpm	131 at 1,800rpm	350 at 2,200rpm
Hp/Wt	17.6	20.6	14.3	15–18	8.1	8.8
Maximum armour	49mm	44mm	76mm	76mm	65mm	102mm
Height (metres)	2.24	2.64	3.02	2.24	2.27	2.45
Main gun	2-pdr (40mm)	37mm	75mm/37mm	75mm	2-pdr (40mm)	6-pdr (57mm)
Main gun rounds	130	103	65/128	90	60	84
Machine guns	1–2 Besa	3–5 .30cal	3 .30cal	2 .30cal, 1 .50cal	1 Besa	2 Besa
Off-road max speed (km/hr)	24	32	18	24–39	15	13
Range on road (km)	322	110	193	163	177	198

Stuarts, Grants and Shermans

In 1941, the first US-produced tank design entered the desert campaign. After the German success in France in 1940, the US moved rapidly to upgrade one of the only designs it had available, the M2A4, into the M3 light tank. As America was also producing the M3 medium tank, the British gave the vehicles names derived from US Civil War generals, and the light M3 became the General Stuart and the M3 mediums Grants or Lees. British tank crews were initially unenthusiastic with the idea of a foreign tank, but the Stuart's smooth ride and reliability soon earned the M3 the nickname 'Honey'. US designers had intended the M3 to serve in the light tank role, but as its firepower, armour and mobility were comparable to the Crusader, it was initially used by the Eighth Army as a cruiser. The Stuart's radial engine gave the tank excellent power and agility, and a top off-road speed of up to 32km/hr. Range was limited to 110km on a single tank of gas, leading British Stuart units to typically stop and fuel, if possible, every 30km. Unlike its British contemporaries, the Stuart was very reliable, rarely shedding its tracks even in poor going and rarely breaking down. If engine repairs were needed, the whole engine could be removed from the rear for maintenance with a simple block and tackle.

The 37mm main gun had an anti-armour performance similar to the 2-pdr's but could also fire small HE shells. Like the Crusader, the Stuart's

By the Second Battle of Alamein, Grants had been joined by the superior M4 Sherman tanks, but were still operated by the 10th Armoured Division's 24th and the 7th Armoured Division's 22nd Armoured Brigades. (Getty Images)

armour was thin, with a maximum of about 44mm. The Stuarts entered battle with coaxial and hull-mounted .30cal Browning machine guns and an additional Browning on the turret in an anti-aircraft mounting. The original design had two additional .30cal machine guns in fixed forward-firing mounts one on each side of the tank over the tracks fired by the driver, but these proved of limited utility and were removed, and the space used for storage. The Stuart was manned by a driver and hull gunner but only had a two-man turret crew, forcing the commander to also serve as gunner. The M3 crew had to shuffle around when the turret rotated while avoiding

M4A1s, known as Sherman IIs in British service, of the 9th Queens, Royal Lancers, 2nd Armoured Brigade, 1st Armoured Division manoeuvre on 5 November 1942. The Shermans had the same chassis as the Grant, but had a lower overall height due to the positioning of the 75mm main gun in a fully rotating turret rather than the Grant's side sponsoon. (Getty Images)

the large drive shaft on the floor, until a turret basket was added with the M3A1 version.

The Stuart debuted in Operation *Crusader,* and fully equipped the 7th Armoured Division's 4th Armoured Brigade. With the arrival of Grants in 1942, at Gazala the 4th Brigade's regiments each had two full Stuart squadrons and one nine-tank Grant squadron. By Alamein, the Stuart was relegated to a light role as more Grants and the first Shermans arrived. The order of battle had 119 Stuarts, with the 7th Armoured Division in the south having most of them in its 4th Light Armoured Brigade. In XXX Corps to the north, the New Zealand's Cavalry Regiment had 25 Stuarts, and the Australian Cavalry had five, along with 15 Crusaders. The Stuart occasionally served in the main battle tank role in Tunisia and, despite the clear obsolescence of its 37mm armament, the Stuart continued to serve through 1945 with Allied forces as a reconnaissance tank and in other specialized roles.

The arrival of the US-built M3 medium in 1942 gave the Eighth Army its first tank with strong reliability and a good balance of mobility, armour and firepower. The design was an improvised one, based on the earlier medium M2A1. The M3 was equipped with the capable 75mm main gun, but as there was no rotating turret design available, it was mounted in a side sponson. A turret was placed atop the tank with a 37mm, making the M3 over three metres tall. The British were desperate to secure more tanks after losses in France and hoped to persuade the US to produce Matildas and Crusaders, but settled for the M3 when no other option was available. They did negotiate some modifications to the original design. As they favoured turret wireless operations, they arranged for US production of a modified 37mm turret elongated to carry the radio and with a coaxial machine gun rather than the original additional small machine-gun turret. These allowed the new version, called the General Grant by the British, to have six rather than seven crewmen as the hull wireless operator was no longer needed. Due to losses, the British did accept some of the original US models – designated General Lees – for service in the desert in 1942.

C

GRANT AND LEE M3 MEDIUM TANKS

1. A Grant tank in the headquarters of the Nottinghamshire Yeomanry, 8th Armoured Brigade, 10th Armoured Division, 23 October 1942. The M3 medium was an interim design as the US lacked a fully rotating turret for the 75mm gun and placed it in a side sponson in the Grant, with a 37mm in a smaller rotating turret above. The resulting design was awkward, with a tank over 3m tall, a large crew and a limited ability to traverse for the 75mm. Despite these shortcomings, the M3 was warmly welcomed by the Eighth Army in 1942 as the 75mm gave British crews their first real ability to match the improved Afrika Korps PzKpfw IIIs and IVs, and even more critically their first tank gun with a good HE shell able to deal with Axis anti-tank guns. The British requested a redesign of the original M3, and as a result the US built 'Grant' variants with a new turret that carried the tank radio behind the 37mm, as was standard in British tanks. This reduced the overall tank crew from seven to six, as no radio operator was required in the main hull.

2. A Lee M3 medium tank. Although the British only planned to use Grant variants of the US M3 medium tank, losses in 1942 led the Eighth Army to be augmented by M3 Lees, and 250 Lees had arrived by June 1942. The Lee's 37mm turret lacked the Grant's radio and featured a smaller additional turret for a .30cal machine gun on top. The tank radio was in the hull and manned by an additional crew member. The tank shown is based on a photograph of a Lee used by the 2nd Armoured Brigade at the First Battle of Alamein in June 1942. The Lee has received a coat of standard sand paint and the sand skirts attached to all US designs before deployment in the desert, but otherwise appears to have been rushed to the front and lacks markings.

1

Robin Hood II
T25016

2

Shermans and Crusaders entering Mersa Matruh during the pursuit of the Afrika Korps after the battle. Most British tank regiments with Shermans had two squadrons with Shermans, and one light squadron with Crusaders. (Getty Images)

The Grant was a reliable vehicle, and even at its fully loaded weight of 26.7 tons had enough engine power for a maximum off-road speed of 18m/hr. Armour was also good for the era and at 76mm was superior to the German PzKpfw IIIs, although the height of the tank and the sponson placement of the 75mm made it difficult to take hull-down positions. The 37mm was actually regarded as the tank's primary anti-tank armament, with the 75mm at last giving an Eighth Army tank an ability to deliver a powerful HE shell against enemy anti-tank guns. The 75mm's initial armour-piercing (AP) round tended to break up on German armour, but later a much more effective round was available when the British captured large numbers of German AP caps and matched them with the US charge.

There were great hopes that the Grants could at last match the PzKpfw IIIs and IVs of the Afrika Korps, but at Gazala the scattered British

D **VALENTINE AND CHURCHILL MK III**

1. A Valentine Mk III of the 50th Royal Tank Regiment, 23rd Armoured Brigade, at Second Alamein. The 50th RTR supported the 51st Highland Division during Operation *Lightfoot*. During early 1942, confidence in British armour collapsed as infantry units were repeatedly overrun by Axis counter-attacks while nearby tank units failed to move up in support. The 23rd Brigade was formed as part of the 8th Armoured Division but trained on Valentines due to limited supplies of cruiser tanks. Rushed to Egypt, the brigade was launched into a disastrous attack during the last days of the First Alamein fighting. Rebuilt, the 23rd was used at Second Alamein in the infantry support role that better suited its Valentine tanks. The 23rd's regiments worked closely with the infantry divisions of XXX Corps throughout the Second Alamein fighting and did much to restore the infantry's faith in the Eighth Army's tankers.

2. A Churchill Mk III of Kingforce, 1st Armoured Division. The British sent six of the new Churchill Mark III Infantry support tanks to North Africa for operational testing and, formed into 'Kingforce' under Major Norris King, they were attached to the 7th Motorized Brigade of the 1st Armoured Division. Advancing during Operation *Supercharge*, one Churchill broke down and another was knocked out, but the others survived numerous hits from enemy anti-tank guns due to their heavy armour. Considered too slow for the pursuit, the Kingforce Churchills departed the theatre after Second Alamein, but Churchills employed in Tunisia in larger numbers proved very successful due to their ability to traverse steep slopes.

1

2

A crew training on a Valentine tank in Britain. The Valentine was designed to replace the Matilda in the infantry support role but, due to a lack of cruiser tanks, equipped several of the armoured divisions forming in Britain in 1941–42, including the Eighth, which arrived in Egypt in the summer of 1942. (Getty Images)

armoured brigades were again defeated in detail by the concentrated panzer divisions. After the catastrophic losses suffered at Knightsbridge, the Eighth Army carefully husbanded its remaining Grants, regarding them as the last hope of halting Rommel at the gates of Egypt. Grants played a major role repelling the last Axis offensive at Alam Halfa; 31 of the 67 tanks knocked out in the action were Grants, but 13 of these were recovered and repaired. By late October, M4 Shermans had arrived in appreciable numbers, but Grants still played a major role at Second Alamein and continued to operate as main battle tanks in Tunisia. Afterwards, the outdated M3s were no longer employed in the front line in the European theatre, although they continued to serve with British and Commonwealth forces in the Far East, in particular during the Burma campaign.

The US M4 Sherman was the dominant Allied tank of World War II, and the best Allied tank in North Africa in 1942. The Sherman used the powertrain and chassis of the M3 Grant, but the hull was redesigned to carry a new fully rotating turret for the 75mm gun. M4s were just beginning to be issued to US armoured units in training when Churchill was informed of the fall of Tobruk in June while visiting the White House and replied to President Roosevelt's offer of aid with the request for 'all the Sherman tanks you can spare'. In response, Shermans were diverted from the 1st US Armoured Division to reinforce the Eighth Army, and despite some losses at sea, 318 arrived at Suez on 11 September along with 100 M7 'Priest' 105mm self-propelled guns.

The Shermans sent to the desert were predominantly M4A1s with a rounded cast hull. The Sherman's balance of mobility, firepower and armour was excellent, and in 1942 could match anything on the Axis side except the Afrika Korps' small numbers of PzKpfw IVs upgraded to carry a long 75mm. The M4 was as rugged and reliable as the Grant and could reach speeds of 39km/hr on good going. Placement of the 75mm in the rotating turret allowed for a lower overall height than the Grant, decreasing vulnerability and improving its ability to fire from hull-down positions. The maximum Sherman armour was 76mm, providing good protection for the era, although enemy guns larger than 50mm could still penetrate it. The Sherman gained a reputation of burning when hit, but, like the Crusader, this was usually due to the ammunition igniting rather than the fuel tank. The M4A1's dual-purpose M3 75mm provided excellent 1942-era firepower, with a capped AP round able to defeat German PzKpfw IIIs and IVs, and an excellent HE shell. The 75mm could fire HE shells out as far as 2,500 metres, allowing British armour to challenge German anti-tank guns at long range. The three-man turret crew allowed for the ideal gunner-loader-commander configuration. A bow gunner manned a .30cal Browning forward next to the driver in the

Crewman cleaning the 2-pdr. The Valentine had a crew of four and featured a three-man turret crew. When up-gunned to carry the 6-pdr after Alamein, the crew was reduced to three, making turret operations inefficient as the commander also had to load the gun, and leaving fewer personnel available for the many daily maintenance and resupply operations needed to keep the tanks operational. (Getty Images)

hull, and another Browning was mounted coaxially with the main gun. A .50cal machine gun was atop the turret in an anti-aircraft mount.

The Shermans were concentrated in the armoured divisions of the X Corps, which had 216 in its order of battle on 23 October. The New Zealand Division's 9th Armoured Brigade received 34 M4s, although the full complement was only issued in early October, leaving the troops little time to train on the new tank. The XIII's 7th Armoured Division had no Shermans and relied on Grants for its secondary attack in the south.

Infantry support tanks

The Matilda was the embodiment of the British pre-war infantry tank concept, slow but heavily armoured. During early engagements with the Italians in 1940, Matildas proved invulnerable to enemy fire but were hindered by the same 2-pdr main armament and poor reliability as the British cruisers. By late 1942, Matildas had almost completely left the Eighth Army's order of battle. The replacement was the Valentine tank, designed to be a more reliable and less expensive version of the Matilda. The Valentine's 65mm frontal armour and small height provided excellent protection, and the tank was well suited to hull-down firing. Its slow speed was considered acceptable due to the tank's infantry support role. The Valentine was fielded with the standard, limited 2-pdr and one coaxial machine gun. It was a small and cramped tank with a

Infantry ride a Valentine into Tripoli during the pursuit of Rommel after Second Alamein. Valentines were soon replaced in British infantry tank brigades with Churchills, but production continued for lend lease purposes as the USSR favoured the Valentine and continued to request more during the last two years of the war. (Getty Images)

three-man turret crew and its diesel engine provided good reliability, a rarity for British-designed tanks in 1942.

The Valentine was fielded in North Africa in infantry support tank brigades during Operation *Crusader* and at Gazala along with the dwindling Matilda force, and due to a lack of cruiser tanks also equipped three of the five armoured divisions forming in Britain in 1942. The 8th Armoured Division was formed in Britain with two brigades equipped with Valentines and was dispatched to the Middle East with them in 1942. The 23rd Brigade arrived first and lost heavily in an ill-considered daylight attack at the end of the First Battle of Alamein. Equipped with new Valentines, 23rd returned to participate in the battle of Alam Halfa and at Second Alamein was attached to the XXX Corps to support its infantry divisions.

An excellent overhead photo of a Churchill infantry support tank. The very first models carried a 3in. howitzer in the bow, but the howitzer was soon replaced by a Besa 7.92 machine gun. (Getty Images)

After Alamein, the Valentine was up-gunned with a 6-pdr. The tank remained well protected, had better firepower, and was reliable, and although it left front-line service with the Western allies, the Soviets considered it one of the best tanks sent via lend-lease, leading to continued production of the Valentine later in the war. The chassis was also used for a variety of other purposes, including the Archer tank destroyer with a 17-pdr gun. In the end, 8,275 Valentines were produced in Britain and Canada, making it the most produced British-designed tank of the war.

 E

MATILDA MK I SCORPION AND A CAMOUFLAGED CRUSADER TANK

1. A Matilda Mk I Scorpion. The Eighth Army had to penetrate the deep minefields laid by their German and Italian opponents, and the Royal Engineers modified 24 obsolete Matilda infantry support tanks to serve as flail tanks to help clear lanes through the mines. A grid structure attached to the Matilda's sides held a rotating drum that would use spinning chains to flail the ground and detonate any anti-tank mines. A Ford V-8 engine to drive the drum and sapper driver were mounted in an armoured cab on the side of the tank visible on the plate. In training, the Scorpions were able to advance when flailing at about 1.5km/hr and clear a nine-foot path. Engineers and infantry followed to check for anything missed and mark the lane. In action during Second Alamein the Scorpions proved less useful, as the V-8 engine overheated rapidly leading to breakdowns, and even when working the Scorpion threw up a tremendous amount of dust and debris that blinded the crew and hindered navigation.

2. A Camouflaged Crusader Tank. The Eighth Army conducted a major denial and deception operation, codenamed *Bertram*, to deceive Rommel as to where the October offensive would be focused. To keep Axis attention on a possible major attack to the south, dummy tanks, vehicles and facilities, including a fake pipeline, were constructed. To the north, the Eighth Army camouflaged the massing tanks of the X Corps as much as possible. This Crusader tank has a standardized cover attached to make it resemble a lorry to Axis air reconnaissance. In addition, this Crusader has its centre three wheels painted black to reinforce the illusion that this is a lorry with front and rear wheels. The deception operation was successful, and German intelligence was unaware of the date of the *Lightfoot* attack, even on 23 October, and for several days after the beginning of the offensive kept mobile forces in reserve in the south.

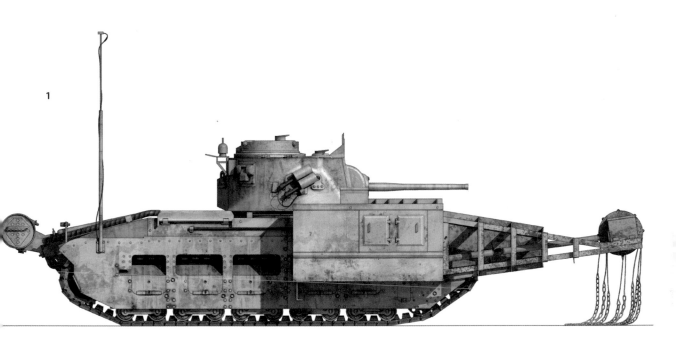

1

2

Kingforce's six Churchills sent to the desert for combat testing. The Churchill detachment was attached to the 1st Armoured Division's 7th Motorized Brigade during the Second Battle of Alamein and engaged enemy positions during Operation *Supercharge*. (Getty Images)

Six new A22 Churchill Mark III infantry support tanks were deployed at Second Alamein for field testing. The Mark I version of the A22 featured heavy armour and a powerful engine, and although a 6-pdr main armament was planned, carried a 2-pdr in the turret as after Dunkirk that was the only weapon available in adequate numbers. A 3in. howitzer was mounted lower in the hull, but as HE rounds for the weapon were in short supply it was generally limited to smoke shells, and the Churchill Mark II exchanged the howitzer for a hull-mounted Besa machine gun. By early 1941, work began to mount a redesigned turret carrying the 6-pdr on the Churchill hull, resulting in the Mark III.

The Churchill was the most successful of the British infantry tank designs of the war and served throughout the remainder of the conflict. It was heavy, at 40 tons, and carried 102mm armour protection in the front hull, slightly more than the German Tiger I, but its 350-horsepower engine gave it reasonable mobility. The Churchill could achieve a speed of 24km/hr, although its unusual suspension made the tank extremely noisy at that speed, so it typically operated at 16km/hr – ideal for its infantry support role – when in action. Churchills proved able to handle the sharp slopes of Tunisia in 1943. The tank had a good crew arrangement, with three manning the turret and two in the hull.

The six Churchill IIIs sent to the Middle East arrived in Egypt on 1 October 1942. After some testing with the Mechanization Experimental Establishment at Cairo, the tanks were sent to the front to participate in

A Matilda modified to serve as a Scorpion minesweeping flail tank. The Scorpions were of limited effectiveness during the Second Alamein offensive, but paved the way for the development of a wide variety of specialized tanks, including Sherman flail tanks, that served with Allied forces for the remainder of the war. (© IWM E 19019)

the Second Alamein offensive later in the month. The six were formed into a special squadron under Major Norris King, designated 'Kingforce', and operated under the control of the 1st Armoured Division's 7th Motorized Brigade during *Supercharge*. One Churchill broke down and one was knocked out by enemy fire, but the others successfully engaged the enemy before two eventually withdrew with non-operational guns.

The Matilda infantry tank had been impervious to enemy fire during the Western Desert Force's rout of the Italians in 1940, but proved vulnerable to the 88mm anti-aircraft gun used in an anti-tank role when the Afrika Korps arrived in early 1941. Few were left in the Eighth Army at Alamein, but a small number were converted to serve as mine-clearing

A good view of the mounting of the armoured side compartments that held the engines and a sapper driver to control the operation of the flail on Matilda minesweeping Scorpion tanks. (© IWM E 18868)

tanks. An additional engine and sapper driver position was mounted in an armoured box mounted on the side of the tank, powering a roller that flailed the terrain in front of the tank with chains to detonate mines and clear a path. The name 'Scorpion' for the vehicle was suggested by the XXX Corps' chief engineer, Brigadier Kenneth Ray, and enthusiastically endorsed by Montgomery, who responded with the biblical quote 'I shall chastise you with scorpions' from the First Book of Kings. The vehicles were prepared by the 21st Field Park Company and 24 were available by 16 October, manned by six officers and 39 other ranks drawn from the 42nd and 44th Royal Tank Regiment. The tank could only make about 1.5km/hr when flailing and generated tremendous clouds of dust. The smoke and noise reportedly terrified one defending Italian unit but choked the crew and made navigation difficult. The flails threw debris, even potentially mines, at the driver if he had the hatch open.

The Scorpions were distributed widely to assist in the *Lightfoot* initial minefield clearing operation but proved of limited effectiveness. In the 7th Armoured Division's secondary assault to the south, the column encountered a stray mine, leading the assigned Scorpions to begin flailing 750m before they reached the edge of the minefield, and their slow flailing speed and the large clouds of dust hindered rather than aided the assault. In the other sectors, the Scorpions tended to overheat, with their air filters unable to deal with the dust clouds, leading to numerous breakdowns despite efforts by the crews to get them moving again. The troubled use of Matilda Scorpions at Second Alamein was, however, followed by a wide variety of specialized tanks developed and used by British forces much more successfully later in the war, including improved mine-clearing Scorpion flail tanks based on Shermans.

THE CAMPAIGN

Montgomery began planning and preparations to take the offensive and, as he announced to the troops, 'knock the enemy for six out of Africa' immediately after the repulse of Rommel's last offensive at Alam Halfa. The Eighth Army faced a sophisticated defensive system, as Rommel realized that the initiative had passed to the British and began to prepare to blunt the coming attack. He considered a mobile defence impracticable due to transport and fuel shortages, and ordered the creation of deep fortified zones. The main feature of his Alamein line was the extensive use of mines. What Rommel called his 'Devil's Gardens' contained about 445,000 anti-tank and 14,000 anti-personnel mines, with booby traps and other obstacles interspersed to hinder clearing operations. Light machine-gun posts ready to call in artillery were at the outer edges and amongst the minefields, with German infantry and anti-tank guns dug in and interspersed with Italian forces down to the battalion level to stiffen them along the main lines of defence.

Montgomery and Rommel both knew that the Panzerarmee's mobile forces were the ultimate key to the defence, and the Eighth Army must engage and destroy them to force the Axis into a retreat. Rommel's forces had 249 German and 278 Italian tanks, along with 20 light tanks. Only a handful of the latest PzKpfw IV armed with the long 75mm gun – the German tank that could best match the Sherman – had reached the panzer divisions. The lack of fuel forced Rommel to place his armoured reserves close to the front, and a mixed battlegroup with the 15th Panzer and Littorio Armoured Divisions was positioned to the north, and the 21st Panzer and Ariete Armoured in the south. The 90th Light and Trieste Motorized Divisions were to the rear, guarding the coast against any amphibious threat. Although Rommel afterwards called Alamein the 'battle without hope', Axis forces had repelled Eighth Army attacks numerous times during the summer and could face Montgomery's offensive with a measure of optimism.

Montgomery planned for Operation *Lightfoot* to begin with a massive night bombardment and four-division infantry assault to open corridors through the Axis minefields. The artillery preparation would begin with 832 25-pdrs and 52 medium guns, with counter-battery fire followed by a rolling barrage ahead of the attacking infantry. The XXX Corps' 9th Australian, 51st Highland, 2nd New Zealand and 1st South African Infantry Divisions would advance behind the barrage, destroy enemy fortified positions and clear a series of lanes through the Axis minefields. The mine-clearing engineer and infantry teams would use some mine detectors and Scorpion flail tanks but would primarily rely on prodding the ground with rods and bayonets. The infantry was to reach an objective line designated 'Oxalic' by the dawn of 24 October.

General Montgomery posing with his Grant tank. Montgomery arrived in the desert in August in a standard British general officer's uniform, but soon adopted a tanker's beret as part of his distinctive public persona. He posed for a number of publicity photos with the Grant, including a picture featured on the cover of *Life* magazine in the United States. (Getty Images)

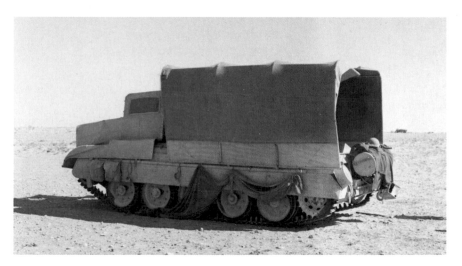

A Crusader tank with a cover to camouflage it as a lorry. Operation *Bertram* was a sophisticated Eighth Army effort to deceive the Axis into assessing that the Allied offensive would be focused on a major attack against the southern portion of their defensive lines. Dummy tanks and equipment were positioned in the XIII Corps area, while the armour of X Corps was camouflaged to look like trucks in the north. (© IWM E 18461)

To protect the lead infantry battalions from panzer counter-attacks, Montgomery insisted that armour closely support the infantry assault. Valentine regiments of the 23rd Armoured Brigade were attached to the Australians, Highlanders and South Africans, and the New Zealand division would attack with its own 9th Armoured Brigade in direct support. Behind the infantry assault, the 1st and 10th Armoured Divisions were to immediately drive forward led by their own specially formed mine-clearing detachments to clear their own divisional lanes. The X Corps tanks were to drive through the infantry on Oxalic and seize an objective line designated 'Pierson'. The armoured divisions would then engage the panzers and shield the XXX Corps divisions as they launched what Montgomery termed 'crumbling attacks' to destroy remaining German and Italian infantry positions. The *Lightfoot* plan was not without its critics, however, and X Corps commander LtGen Lumsden and other armour officers felt moving the armour through the minefields on the first night was too ambitious, and warned their subordinates to be leery of charging dug-in German anti-tank guns.

British forces mounted a major deception effort – Operation *Bertram* – to convince Axis intelligence that the major Eighth Army attack would take place in the south rather than the north. In addition to false radio traffic, the British constructed thousands of dummy tanks, trucks and logistical installations in the XIII Corps area to indicate another armoured division was located there along with the 7th. A dummy pipeline was laid moving towards the south, but carefully shown to aerial reconnaissance to be incomplete to convince the enemy that any attack was still weeks away. The XIII's 7th Armoured Division would launch a secondary attack in the south as part of *Bertram*, although Montgomery directed that Horrocks be sure to limit any tank losses and maintain readiness to deploy north if needed. At the same time, *Bertram* took additional measures to disguise the X Corps' armour massing in the north. Lorries were openly parked near the front, and the armoured units were held farther to the rear. As the time for the attack neared, the tanks were moved up during the night and replaced the trucks with 'sunshields' that made tanks and limbered artillery look like lorries from the air. Axis intelligence reported the enemy situation to be unchanged on the eve of the attack, and Rommel was on medical leave in Germany and only recalled to the desert at noon on the second day of the offensive.

British Grant crew cleaning the barrel of the top turret's 37mm. Montgomery insisted on delaying the Eighth Army offensive until late October to allow for more time for re-equipping, reorganizing and, in particular, training. (Getty Images)

The assault: 23 October 1942

Operation *Lightfoot* began at 2140hrs on 23 October with the planned massive barrage followed closely by the attacking infantry and Valentine tanks of the XXX Corps. Although they did not completely close to the Oxalic objective line, the infantry divisions were able to make strong progress except for one brigade of the 51st Highland which lagged due to the length of the assigned frontage. The advance of the 1st and 10th Armoured Divisions was more troubled, with slow mine-clearing, surviving Axis outposts, and smoke and dust leading to huge traffic jams in their crowded, narrow lanes. The 1st Armoured advanced to open its assigned lane between the 9th Australian and 51st Highland Divisions in the north but had not reached the infantry by daylight. To the south, the 10th Armoured made better progress and by dawn the lead elements of its 8th Armoured Brigade joined the New Zealand Division's 9th Armoured behind Miteirya Ridge. Throughout the day, attempts by British tanks to push through the infantry and reach the Pierson objective line stalled in the face of enemy anti-tank gun fire, and any British tanks that crested Miteirya Ridge were rapidly hit. Much of the X

 SHERMAN M4A1

A Sherman M4A1 medium tank, 9th (Queen's Own) Lancers, 2nd Armoured Brigade, 1st Armoured Division. The arrival of Sherman tanks in the autumn of 1942 gave the Eighth Army large numbers of a tank that outmatched any Axis tank at the battle except small numbers of PzKpfw IVs upgraded with a long 75mm gun. The Sherman had an excellent balance of firepower, mobility and armour, and was notable for its high mechanical reliability. This Sherman displays the camouflage pattern of dark green over sand used on most British tanks at Second Alamein, and the variety of specialized markings often applied to British vehicles in World War II. The right front fender carries the 1st Armoured Division white rhino formation sign, the red square on the left indicates the senior brigade in the division, and '86' indicates the 9th Lancers. The same markings are carried on the rear fenders. The circle on the turret is intended to allow the regimental commander to rapidly identify the tank's squadron in action – a diamond for the headquarters, triangle for first, square for second and circle for third squadron. There were variations in the placement and use of all of these markings, and some were obscured before action. The arrival in battle of replacement or repaired tanks also led to a variety of markings being seen in battle.

Grant tanks replenished and ready for operations photographed on 27 October 1942. Two armoured brigades – the 22nd and 24th – were heavily equipped with Grants for the offensive, and the 9th operated approximately a regiment's worth of Grants along with Crusaders and Shermans. (© IWM E 18532)

Corps' combat power remained stalled in traffic jams in the narrow minefield lanes, taking losses to artillery fire.

Command confusion ensued as Lumsden, Leese and the various armoured and infantry divisional commanders attempted to gain control of their units and push forward. Montgomery repeatedly ordered X Corps to attack more aggressively and gain the Pierson objective line without regard to losses. Lumsden attempted to comply, but command and control problems at corps and division level and the fire from German anti-tank guns halted any attempt to advance, leaving Montgomery convinced the British armour and its commanders lacked 'pep'.

But while British tanks failed to advance as planned, they inflicted heavy losses on the Panzerarmee's mobile reserves moving to counter-attack on the morning of the 24th. The Axis forces moved to employ their standard tactics of engaging the British armour at long range but were stunned to receive effective return fire from the 75mm guns of the X Corps Shermans. Even the deadly 88s could be hit by Shermans lobbing HE rounds at long range. The Desert Air Force, 105mm Priest self-propelled guns, infantry 2- and 6-pdr anti-tank guns, and Eighth Army artillery all joined in battering the Axis forces, and by 25 October the 15th Panzer Division reported that only 31 of its original force of 119 tanks were still operational.

Reset and 'dog fight'

By the third day of the offensive, it became clear that despite the damage inflicted on the enemy, the *Lightfoot* attack was bogged down. In the south, the 7th Armoured Division penetrated the first enemy minefield but stalled in front of the main defensive line, and Montgomery ordered the diversionary attack cancelled to limit losses. To the north, XXX and X Corps

Shermans of the 8th Armoured Brigade being readied for a renewed advance 27 October 1942. Several days into the attack, Montgomery concluded that *Lightfoot* had failed to achieve a breakthrough and withdrew the 2nd New Zealand and 1st and 10th Armoured Divisions to reconstitute a reserve for a new attack. (© IWM E 18531)

were holding off and steadily attritting the Panzerarmee's mobile reserves, but British tanks were still pinned down short of the original Pierson objective line. The initial phase of the offensive had cost the Eighth Army 191 tanks, 122 of these Grants or Shermans, but 40 to 50 tanks were repaired and returned daily. To keep the offensive going, Montgomery ordered the 9th Australian Division supported by 23rd Brigade Valentines to clear the Axis defences to the north, shielded by the tanks and infantry along the front.

As the Australian attack ground forward, X Corps launched some limited objective attacks to improve its positions to its front. During the night of 26/27 October, the 7th Motorized Brigade moved forward to seize several objectives near Kidney Ridge. The attacking units became disoriented during the night attack, but by morning the 2nd Battalion of the rifle brigade with 19 6-pdr anti-tank guns was positioned holding a slight depression known as Snipe. The next day, the battalion held off repeated enemy attacks at great cost, knocking out over 50 German and Italian tanks. The 24th Armoured Brigade, however, failed to move up and support the beleaguered force, at one point taking their own troops on Snipe under fire.

A burning Grant tank. Although it had good armour, the Grant's height and difficulties effectively using hull-down positions increased its vulnerability to enemy fire. (Getty Images)

Operation *Supercharge*

Montgomery now gathered forces for a renewed breakthrough operation to be designated *Supercharge*. The 2nd New Zealand Division was shifted into reserve and its 9th Armoured Brigade received priority for replacement tanks. The 10th Armoured Division and its 24th Brigade were pulled from the action due to losses, and the 10th's 8th Armoured Brigade shifted to the 1st Armoured Division to strengthen it for the new attack. The 7th Armoured Division was pulled from the south to serve as an additional reserve directly under Eighth Army control.

Eighth Army Grant, Sherman and Crusader strength for Operation *Supercharge*				
Unit	Grants	Shermans	Crusader IIIs	Crusader IIs
9th Armoured Brigade	40	39	24	29
1st Armoured Division				6
2nd Armoured Brigade		90	26	40
8th Armoured Brigade	39	23	20	27
7th Armoured Division				4
22nd Armoured Brigade	54		10	18
Totals	**133**	**152**	**80**	**124**

The new push would resemble *Lightfoot* but with a smaller force concentrated on a narrower, 3,500m front just north of Miteirya Ridge. Freyberg was placed in command of the attack, and Montgomery gave him the 151st Brigade of the 50th Division and 152nd of the 51st Highland to lead the assault as New Zealand infantry replacements were in short supply.

Crusaders photographed on 26 October manoeuvring towards enemy lines through a gap cleared in the Axis minefields. (© IWM E 18479)

The attack was again to take place at night, with 192 guns firing a creeping barrage in front of the advancing infantry and 168 hitting deeper and flank targets. Valentines of the 23rd Armoured Brigade supported the two-brigade attack. The rebuilt 9th Armoured Brigade was to follow closely and rapidly thrust through the infantry just before dawn to destroy enemy anti-tank guns 1,800m deeper, with the 1st Armoured Division with the 2nd and 8th Armoured and 7th Motorized Brigades to follow closely to exploit the gap.

Supercharge began during the night of 2 November. The barrage and infantry assault went well, as there were fewer mines to deal with, and the infantry reached most of their objectives by the early morning hours. With some difficulty, the 9th Armoured followed behind the attacking troops. Montgomery had told brigade commander BrigGen J.C. Currie that he would accept 100 per cent losses in the 9th if necessary to hold a door open for the breakout of the following 1st Armoured Division. The plan called

A US-made M7 Priest self-propelled 105mm howitzer passes a destroyed enemy tank. In addition to Sherman tanks, the US shipped 100 M7s to the 8th Army, where they operated alongside British Bishop self-propelled 25-pdrs mounted on a Valentine tank chassis. (Getty Images)

for the 9th to attack under cover of darkness and destroy the enemy anti-tank gun positions along the Rahman Track, but with one regiment late in reaching the start line the assault was delayed half an hour, and dawn was breaking behind the tanks as the regiments crossed their start lines.

The 9th attacked with the 3rd Hussars to the north, Royal Wiltshire Yeomanry in the centre and Warwickshire Yeomanry in the south, with a total of 133 Grants, Shermans and Crusaders. The faster Crusaders were able to get to the Rahman Track while it was still dark, machine gunning, charging and crushing German infantry and gun positions. The Shermans and Grants trailed behind and took heavy losses to 88mm guns positioned behind the track as they were silhouetted against the rising sun. Ultimately, 102 of the tanks that had begun the attack were knocked out with 31 officers and 198 men lost; 35 German tanks and guns were destroyed in turn. The German defences had been damaged and dented, but not destroyed.

Unfortunately, the 9th Armoured Brigade's sacrifice did not lead to an immediate breakthrough. The 1st Armoured Division's advance was led by a reconstituted mine-clearing detachment with the engineers covered by a motor battalion and three troops of Crusaders followed by the 2nd Armoured, 7th Motorized and 8th Armoured. The Kingforce Churchill tank detachment advanced attached to the 7th. As the 1st emerged on the front line, it was greeted by the sight of the 9th's destroyed tanks, and divisional commander MajGen Raymond Briggs handled his unit cautiously, ordering his division to take hull-down positions amongst the anti-tank guns of the attached motorized battalions.

The most sustained clash of armour at Second Alamein ensued as Rommel launched counter-attacks with all his mobile divisions against the salient driven by *Supercharge* into his final line of defence. The 2nd Armoured Brigade emerged on the front line first, and 35 surviving tanks of the 9th were formed into a composite regiment and posted to its north. The 8th Armoured followed and covered the southern flank. Shortly after 0900hrs, the 15th and 21st Panzer Divisions moved to attack, but as on the day after *Lightfoot*, their attempts to achieve fire superiority at long range were met with intense shelling from the Sherman 75s and Priest self-propelled 105mm howitzers, and any attempt to press home their attack was unable to shift the British.

G   **THE ATTACK OF THE 9TH ARMOURED BRIGADE, OPERATION *SUPERCHARGE*, 2 OCTOBER 1942.**

The artillery and infantry portion of *Supercharge* was to be immediately followed by an assault by B.G. Currie's 9th Armoured Brigade to break open Axis defences and allow the next formation, the 1st Armoured Division, to exploit the breach and break out. The 9th's tanks were to attack before dawn, advance about 2,000yds and destroy enemy anti-tank positions around the Rahman Track. Currie had expressed concern about the vulnerability of his tanks to enemy fire due to the lessons of previous Eighth Army disasters, but Montgomery persisted and stated he would accept one hundred percent losses to keep the momentum of the attack going. The infantry assault went well, but the 9th's tanks had difficulties moving through the remaining minefields, and Currie held the attack for a critical half hour to allow the Warwickshire Yeomanry to arrive on the start line. The tanks moved off as dawn was breaking, with the 3rd Hussars to the north, the Wiltshire Yeomanry in the centre and the Warwickshire Yeomanry to the south. The faster Crusaders were able to drive forward rapidly and begin to engage the enemy anti-tank guns with machine guns and physically ram and overrun the positions. The following Shermans and Grants, however, were silhouetted against the rising sun and took heavy losses to 50mm and 88mm anti-tank guns. The battlescene shows one of the faster Crusaders knocked out to the left, and the Shermans and Grants suffering from enemy anti-tank fire. The 9th was able ultimately to hold the Rahman Track and destroy a number of anti-tank positions, but at the cost of 102 of their 128 tanks. The following 1st Armoured Division, sobered by the large number of burning British tanks, took up defensive positions along with the remnants of Currie's brigade. The anticipated *Supercharge* breakthrough was delayed, but counter-attacking Axis armour suffered crippling losses during the next day trying to seal off the dent driven in their last line of defence.

M4A1 Shermans advancing on 5 November after the Eighth Army breakthrough. The pursuit was hindered by traffic control problems, rain, and mines and booby traps left by the retreating Axis forces. (© IWM E 18971)

The 2nd Armoured Brigade reported 25 enemy tanks destroyed to its front and, by the end of the day, the Panzerarmee had lost another estimated 70 German and 45 Italian tanks.

Although *Supercharge* had not produced a clean breakthrough, the attrition of Axis forces had reached catastrophic levels, and the DAK reported only 24 operational tanks on 3 November. Rommel began preparations for a systematic withdrawal, but Hitler dispatched a message demanding the Panzerarmee stand fast, stunning Rommel and throwing Axis forces into confusion. On the night of 3/4 November, the Eighth Army mounted another series of infantry and artillery assaults that finally broke through the last Axis defence lines, and armoured cars moved through to begin harassing the retreating enemy forces. When Rommel decided to issue a clear order to withdraw later on the 4th, it was too late for the bulk of the Axis forces fighting on the Alamein line. All the infantry and the greater part of the Italian XX Mechanized Corps were lost, and DAK commander General Wilhelm Ritter von Thoma was captured during the chaotic rush to escape.

The Eighth Army's pursuit after Alamein encountered numerous difficulties. British preparations had focused on training and planning for battling through the Axis minefields rather than pursuit, and most units, including X Corps, had been heavily engaged for days and needed to resupply and reorganize. The 8th Armoured Brigade returned to the 10th Division, and, along with the 1st and 7th, joined the chase. The 4th Light Armoured Brigade was shifted to Freyberg's New Zealanders to replace the heavily damaged 9th Armoured. A series of British armoured hooks through the desert failed to capture the retreating enemy, and weather, mines, booby traps and traffic control problems ultimately allowed Rommel to escape. Key German command, staff and support elements were able to withdraw, covered by a rear guard with the surviving combat elements – roughly the equivalent of a regimental battlegroup. The Operation

Captured German armour collected from the Alamein battlefield. Key headquarters and command personnel escaped the Eighth Army pursuit, but the vast majority of the Panzerarmee's combat power was destroyed or captured during Second Alamein fighting. (© IWM E 26958)

Torch landings on 8 November meant that the Axis position in Africa was ultimately doomed. Hitler poured in large reinforcements to hold a bridgehead in Tunisia that prolonged the campaign but ultimately led to the loss of 267,000 Axis troops in May 1943.

ASSESSMENT AND IMPLICATIONS

The Second Battle of Alamein devastated Rommel's Panzerarmee. The Axis lost 55,000 troops, 30,000 of them prisoners, along with 1,000 guns and 450 tanks. With the loss of the battlefield, the German and Italian forces were unable to recover and repair disabled tanks. The cost to the Eighth Army was also high, with 13,500 casualties and 500 tanks knocked out. As many of these were disabled by mines and the British had made major strides in their ability to recover and repair tanks, 350 returned to service.

The Eighth Army attack had not gone to plan but had ultimately battered the Axis into defeat through a grinding battle of attrition. The *Lightfoot* and *Supercharge* night infantry attacks, superbly supported by artillery and engineers, had been able to penetrate Rommel's deep Devil's Gardens minefields. The 23rd Armoured Brigade's Valentine-equipped regiments performed well in support of the XXX Corps infantry and did much to restore trust between foot soldiers and tankers. The 1st and 10th Armoured Divisions of Montgomery's specially formed X Corps' *corps de chasse*, however, proved unable to rapidly penetrate the minefields and attack through the infantry the next morning as per the *Lightfoot* plan. Similarly, despite the sacrifice of the 9th Armoured Brigade's attack during *Supercharge*, the 1st Armoured Division's tanks were unable to make a clean breakthrough and were held up by the deep Axis anti-tank defences. But while the breakthrough remained elusive, Montgomery's plans had ensured that British tanks were present to support the infantry and defeat the inevitable panzer counter-attacks.

Eighth Army Stuarts on the Benghazi waterfront, December 1942. Although British units were unable to capture the remnants of the Afrika Korps, Montgomery ensured the pursuit was strongly supported logistically, and Rommel was unable to launch another counter-attack from El Agheila as he had in early 1941 and 1942. (Getty Images)

An M3 Lee tank at the battle of Imphal-Kohima. Obsolete in Europe, the M3 served on in the Far East, where its reliability and strong frontal armour made it useful as it generally operated head-on on narrow trails against Japanese fortified positions, and a fully rotating turret for the 75mm main gun was not missed. (Getty Images)

Now, British tanks, artillery and anti-tank guns were able to inflict heavy losses on Rommel's counter-attacking mobile reserves. The 75mms of the Shermans and Grants proved particularly deadly and were able to take the DAK's panzers – long used for pummelling Allied positions from long range and goading British tanks into costly charges – themselves under effective fire.

The British armoured divisions made a critical contribution to the victory, but they still faced difficulties with effective combined arms manoeuvres. The initial move through the minefields on the night of 23/24 October by the 1st, 7th and 10th Armoured Divisions failed to reach their objectives, and Montgomery would subsequently relieve several of the old desert hands, including X Corps commander Lumsden. Montgomery's *corps de chasse* concept was abandoned, and after Second Alamein the Eighth Army typically combined armoured and infantry divisions in each corps command. At the division level, armoured and motorized or lorried infantry brigades often operated separately and had difficulties supporting one another. During the 1st Armoured Division's operations at Snipe on 27 October, the 24th Armoured Brigade failed to reach and support the besieged motorized battalion and mistakenly fired on their own troops. As late as 1944, British armoured divisions landing in Normandy still planned to use their lorried and armoured brigades for separate tactical tasks, with the infantry to assault and hold objectives while the armour brigade was to be used only for exploitation. Under the pressure of fighting in France, the divisions soon turned to better combined arms techniques with each armoured regiment paired with one of the division's infantry battalions in balanced combined arms teams.

Second Alamein was notable for the debut of the tanks that British forces would use for the remainder of the war. The Sherman was superior to all opponents in 1942 except the PzKpfw IV with a long 75mm. Although it was subsequently out-gunned by German tanks, the Sherman remained the dominant tank in Allied service due to its reliability, ease of production and delays in the production of a heavy tank to match the Panthers and Tigers. Stuarts soldiered on in reconnaissance units until the end of the war despite their weak armour and 37mm main gun, some in 1944–45 with turrets removed and additional machine guns fitted. The Churchill, tested in small numbers at Alamein, became the predominant infantry support tank used by British and Commonwealth forces. The earlier tanks in the force at Alamein, including the Crusaders and Grants, remained in combat throughout the Tunisian campaign but were replaced by Shermans before the invasion of Sicily in July. Crusader chassis were converted to other purposes, particularly anti-aircraft tanks, and Grants continued to serve in Burma and in the Pacific. Even the troubled Matilda Scorpion was followed by a wide variety of specialized armoured vehicles operated by the 79th Armoured Division – under Percy Hobart – that supported Allied operations from D-Day to the Rhine.

FURTHER READING

Doctrine and tactics

Doherty, R., *British Armoured Divisions and Their Commanders, 1939–1945* (Pen & Sword Military, 2013)

French, D., *Raising Churchill's Army: The British Army and the War Against Germany 1919–1945* (Oxford University Press, 2000)

Griffith, P., *Desert Tactics in World War II* (Osprey Elite 162, 2008)

Moreman, T., *Desert Rats: British Eighth Army in North Africa, 1941–43* (Osprey Battle Orders 28, 2007)

Order of battle

Hughes, D., J. Broshot and A. Philson, *The British Armies in World War Two: An Organizational History, Volume One: British Armoured and Cavalry Divisions* (George F. Nafziger, 1999)

Hughes, D., D. Ryan and S. Rothwell, *The British Armies in World War Two: An Organizational History, Volume Four: British Tank and Armoured Brigades* (George F. Nafziger, 2002)

Joslen, H.F., *Orders of Battle, Second World War 1939–45* (London Stamp Exchange, 1990)

Perrett, B., *British Tanks in North Africa, 1940–42* (Osprey Vanguard 23, 1981)

Robins, C., 'Orders of Battle of British Tank Forces, and Tank Types at Key Dates in the Western Desert, 1940–42', *Journal of the Society for Army Historical Research*, spring 2015, Vol. 93, No. 373, pp. 48–59, Society for Army Historical Research, Stable URL: https://www.jstor.org/stable/4423267

Technical factors

Fletcher, D., *British Battle Tanks: British-Made Tanks of World War II* (Osprey, 2018)

Fletcher, D., and S. Zaloga, *British Battle Tanks: American-Made World War II Tanks* (Osprey, 2018)

Perrett, B., *The LEE/GRANT Tanks in British Service* (Osprey Vanguard 6, 1978)

Perrett, B., *The Stuart Light Tank Series* (Osprey Vanguard 17, 1980)

The battle

Bungay, S., *Alamein* (Aurum, 2002)

Ford, K., *El Alamein 1942: The Turning of the Tide* (Osprey Campaign 158, 2005)

Latimer, J., *Alamein* (Harvard University Press, 2002)

Tank markings and paint schemes

Hodges, P., *British Military Markings 1939–1945* (Almark Publications, 1971)

Platz, W., *Desert Tracks: British Armour Camouflage and Markings in North Africa* (Baron Publishing Company, 1978)

Taylor, D., *Warpaint: Colours and Markings of British Army Vehicles 1993–2003, Volume 2* (Mushroom Model Publications, 2009)

White, B.T., *British Tank Markings and Names* (Squadron Publications, Inc, 1978)

INDEX

Page numbers in **bold** refer to illustrations with some caption locators in brackets. Page numbers in *italic* refer to tables.